Hinduism

An Essential Guide to Understanding Hinduism and the Hindu Religion, Including Beliefs, Rituals, Holidays, and the Process of Converting to Hinduism

by Reena George

Table of Contents

Introduction

Hinduism originated in India – the land of diverse ethnicity and culture. However, amidst this diversity, Hindus try to promote peace and universality of shared beliefs. Diversity and communal unity, irrespective of faith, also apply to their religious practices. As Hinduism has spread its wings, various versions of the religion sprang from different groups around the world. So, to be able to understand Hinduism, you should first know that it's not just a religion, but also considered a way of life.

Among experts, present-day Hinduism is widely considered to be a sum total of many traditions, rituals, and customs originating from multiple Indian cultures through the centuries. It is, therefore, a rather unifying religion, which gathers followers from varying backgrounds around a few central notions and spiritual goals that are universal to all Hindus. Quite unlike some other prominent religions, Hinduism has seen much development and many changes and has come a long way since its ancient origins.

There is no strict and universal declaration of rules and guidelines to being a Hindu. Rather, Hinduism brings together many denominations, cultures and philosophies under its umbrella, which is also the way scholars usually describe Hinduism in the first place – an umbrella term covering an array of beliefs and practices that all share a few core principles and have been fused together since before our era.

The synthesis, or fusion of Hinduism, as many experts explain its formation, started to occur between the year 800 BCE and 300 CE. Before this process began, the most common form of faith was the Vedic religion, which is traced back to around the year 1750 BCE. This old religion is itself considered in our times as the first era of the development and shaping of Hinduism, thus earning Hinduism the title of the oldest existing religion in the world.

This evolution is generally explained as a gradual, cultural process that went on as more and more cultures started to gather around the key beliefs that would come to define Hinduism. The religion itself, therefore, has no founders and is rooted in multiple sources and philosophies. The nature of its formation has also made Hinduism one of the most complex and diverse religious practices in the world. The spread of the religion well beyond its native grounds has also additionally enriched and expanded the philosophy.

Thanks to the fact that the Indian people are present in almost all corners of the globe in at least some number, Hinduism has been disseminated far and wide through much of the world. Another contributing factor is perhaps the historical contact with the West, especially during colonial times. Either way, Hinduism is a well-established and popular religion, with a followership of well over one billion worshippers worldwide, most of who are in India. Nepal, Bangladesh, and Bali are also home to millions of Hindus. Among the western countries in the developed world, the United States and the United Kingdom have the largest numbers of the religion's followers.

Hinduism has been the object of much interest within many countries and civilizations for ages and continues to attract attention well into the modern era. Many people are seeking to integrate the Hindu practices into their everyday lives for a variety of reasons. The practice of this religion in the developed world or, more importantly, the adaptation of certain aspects and teachings of it in modern life is a testament to its popularity and reach.

One reason for its popularity is the fact that it's the oldest known religion in the world, with its history reportedly dating back as far as 6500 B.C.E. It's not the only religion in India, but it is the most predominant. Therefore, if nothing else, being the third largest religion in the world definitely makes Hinduism worth knowing about.

Because Hinduism is so broad and complex, this book has been specifically designed to present you with an easy-to-understand overview of this incredible religion. Throughout the following chapters, I'm going to outline the common beliefs, rituals, holidays, and the overarching concepts that you may wish to apply to your own life, should you choose to follow Hinduism.

As I have mentioned, Hinduism is a religion with a wide range of denominations, sects, scriptures, and cultural backgrounds. What defines a set of beliefs as a Hindu practice are the specific, fundamental notions concerning human life, spirituality, and the nature of our universe. Within all denominations that classify as Hindu, you will find a common pattern. In our first chapter, we will look into the basic beliefs that bring together the many diversities under Hinduism.

Whatever your motivation to learn about Hinduism may be – whether you're just curious to learn what makes this religion different from others, or whether you're perhaps planning to convert – you've come to the right place. By the end of this book, you'll have a firm grasp on the core of this historic system of faith. And in case you are considering converting to Hinduism, this book will disclose the essential aspects of conversion, and it will show you the recommended steps for how to go about the process.

Chapter 1: The Major Beliefs and Practices of Hinduism

Although Hinduism has turned into a conglomerate of varied faith-based philosophies classed under a single umbrella term, there are still major beliefs and practices that are observed by most Hindus. Most of these major beliefs usually revolve around the following principles.

Your Karma will affect your life

Karma is a well-known concept in many philosophies as well as popular culture. As pertaining to spirituality, mainly in Hinduism, Karma represents a connection between an individual's actions in life and his circumstances in this life or the next, relative to different schools of thought. These circumstances are seen as direct consequences of the individual's actions and deeds. As for the term itself, it is rooted in Sanskrit and directly translates to "action" or "deed". The concept of Karma predates the fusion of Hinduism and is traced back to the original Vedic religion.

Apart from the religious notions of Karma, this concept can be observed as a natural course of events too. In particular, certain actions will bring about specific consequences, which can be predicted with accuracy. For example, reckless driving is irresponsible and unjust to other drivers in the traffic, and your personal injury or something worse is a very likely outcome if you behave in this manner. That is what Karma is in essence, a system of cause and effect that occurs without divine intervention all the time. Therefore, it can be argued that the concept may have origins which don't necessarily pertain to religion, but are rather found in regular, everyday wisdom. Regardless, the notion of Karma is heavily extrapolated and represented in Hinduism and other religions, and it is one of the crucial principles of these philosophies.

This belief doesn't only prompt one to conduct themselves morally and do good but also offers an explanation for the hardships of life. Hindus widely believe that a hard life of poverty or other misfortune is the result of that person's actions in their previous life – immoral actions to be precise. Therefore, if a disadvantaged person commits to leading a life of kindness and good moral choices, he can expect to be rewarded and change his destiny.

Hindus believe that there are two forms of Karma — the good kind which begets "punya" (merit, good, virtue, etc.), and the bad kind that leads to "paap" (demerit, sin, etc.). If you have done good deeds in your previous life, this can come back to you as rewards in your present one; and that's true with bad Karma too. It's believed that the life you lead in the present is affected by the way you led your life in the past. Essentially, you reap what you sow. Hence, a person can be reincarnated as a human being or an animal depending on his past life. Even within those categories, whether a person is reborn as a human in a prosperous, loving, virtuous home, or one in a run-down household of sin and sorrow, depends on the soul's past Karma as well.

Seeing as the cycle of rebirth is one of the key notions of the Hindu religion, Karma is among the most important aspects of life, to which devout Hindus dedicate much effort and energy during their lives. This is what guides a virtuous Hindu on a moral path and serves as a great source of motivation to hundreds of millions of people to do good unto others.

Reincarnation exists

This is a belief that people's souls are reincarnated in order to continue achieving perfection. Hindus believe that all living things have souls that are eternal. When a person dies, his body dies but not his soul. This soul can transform into a new entity through another vessel, because every soul is a part of "Parmatma", the Supreme Soul. This process occurs repeatedly through the cycle of rebirth until the soul achieves perfection and is freed.

This soul is otherwise referred to as one's "Atman" within Hindu teachings. The Atman is the real self or the very essence of an individual, and it is immortal. According to Hinduism, the soul never dies but merely moves on to a different physical embodiment when it is reincarnated. This form of the recurring rebirth of an individual is a recognized spiritual, or rather existential, process in Hinduism and is referred to as Samsara.

The concepts of Samsara and good or bad Karma are paramount to the way Hindus live their lives. The end goal of a soul's existence, according to Hindu philosophies, is to complete its process of purification through good Karma in the course of the many lives

12

it leads, ultimately becoming free from Samsara and finding salvation.

The Supreme Being can incarnate in human forms

Hindu Veda scriptures state that there's only one God, Brahman (Purusha, The One, Atman), who can manifest or incarnate into other divine as well as mortal forms. This is primarily the reason why Hindus have a dizzying pantheon of gods which are revered, starting with the most prominent ones forming the Big Three – Brahma, Vishnu, and Shiva. These are followed by thousands of other deities, each signifying a particular aspect of the Supreme Being or the lesser gods of the divine pantheon, such as creator, ruler, warrior, scholar, nurturer, etc.

Dashavatara denotes the incarnation of the Lord Vishnu into 10 mortal forms when the Dharma on earth is threatened by human sins. The 10 human forms of Lord Vishnu include Krishna, Ram, Kalki Avatar, Matsyavatar, Narsimhavatar, Kurmavatar, Buddha, Parshuram, Varahavatar, and Vamanavatar. Other deities, such as Shiva or Maa Parvati can also incarnate into human forms.

An interesting thing to note is that certain schools of thought within Hinduism practice the worship of a singular god, but at the same time, they don't necessarily deny belief to others. This is less than rare across different Hindu philosophies, and it is for this reason that Hinduism often gets the label of being a henotheistic religion. Henotheism means exactly that; a devotion to one god while acknowledging the possibility that other gods and deities may exist as well.

All of this further illustrates how diverse Hinduism really is and serves to paint a picture of a rather open-minded religion. The lack of a strict dogma that is enforced and adhered to allows for functional relations between different cultures that contribute their own philosophies and wisdom to the overall religion, thus not only enriching its teachings but strengthening peace and unity as well. One could argue that this nature of Hinduism was one of the deciding factors in making the faith stand the test of time and survive to become the oldest living religious practice.

The goal of the human soul is salvation

The human soul lives repeatedly through death and rebirth in the cycle of reincarnation until perfection is attained for the soul's salvation. Since the individual soul was once a part of the Supreme Soul, it gains oneness with the Supreme Being after salvation is achieved through cycles of good deeds leading to enlightenment. This is the end goal of the human soul.

Through adherence to certain responsibilities and codes of conduct (Dharma), as well as through improving their Karma, a devout Hindu carries on his process of purification, over the course of many lifetimes. Samsara is a cycle which may last indefinitely and go on as long as an individual soul requires in order to be cleansed.

The Hindu understanding of the cycle of rebirth and liberation of one's soul is interesting to contemplate due to the fact that it doesn't profess that a soul will be damned for an eternity if it does evil in its current life. Leading a life of immorality, debauchery, and low virtue will make an individual's next life living hell, yes, but with that new life comes a new opportunity to turn the soul's fate around and return to the path towards liberation. What this means is that "hell" can be escaped, and it means that a soul will be able to find salvation in the end, no matter how sinful the individual may have been and no matter how long the Samsara goes on. Ultimately, some will have to work harder than others, but salvation is within everybody's reach if they focus their energy on it, and it will come in this life or one of the subsequent ones.

Aside from the major beliefs, the following are important concepts that you will want to know about Hinduism.

There are 7 key Hindu scriptures

These scriptures are considered the source of sacred teachings and source of reading materials for Hindus. The seven key Hindu scriptures include Bhagavad Gita, Vedas, Upanishadas, Brahmanas, Puranas, Smritis, and Aranyakas. These, in turn, contain a number of Hindu scriptures, respectively.

In the early days of Hinduism, the teachings and the philosophies of the scriptures were not in written form yet. Instead, they were mostly contained in memory and taught to others verbally. Thus they were passed down the generations in this way for a long time before being recorded in writing.

Hindu scriptures that date all the way back to the beginning are categorized as Shruti and Smriti, and the wisdom contained within them was reformed and enriched many times before they were written down. Revisions and expansions are especially common for the Smriti scriptures.

The Shruti scriptures, which mostly pertain to Vedas, represent the earliest wisdom that was carried on through the generations verbally. Literally translated, Shruti means "that which is heard." Four Vedas fall under Shruti scriptures, and those are Rigveda, Yajurveda, Samaveda, and Atharvaveda. In turn, every one of the four Vedas is cut down into four primary bodies of text, or scriptures.

The four texts found in each of the Vedas are Samhitas, Aranyakas, Brahmanas, and Upanishads. Each of these forms of text speaks on a specific subject. The Samhitas contain writings on various Hindu mantras and benedictions, while the Aranyakas touch upon sacrifices, ceremonies, and other rituals. The texts in the Brahmanas are on the subject of sacrifices and rituals as well. Finally, the Upanishads are philosophical in their contents, with reference to spiritual enlightenment and methods of meditation as well. For this reason, the Upanishads are some of the most important scriptures in the Hindu religion.

On the other hand, the Smriti writings had always been written down and have actual authors. While having much importance on their own, the Smriti scriptures are still not held in as high of an importance as the Shruti texts across different cultures throughout Hinduism.

These particular scriptures consist of various Hindu epics as well as the Puranas, which is a genre or term that encapsulates many ancient myths and stories collected through the many centuries of Hindu practice and philosophy. As for the epics, these are made up of the Ramayana and the Mahabharata. Within the Mahabharata writings, the Bhagavad Gita stands out as one of the most prominent Hindu writings in history.

There are various thoughts and sects within Hinduism

As I have previously mentioned, Hinduism is one of the most diverse and complex religious practices. While this can be a confusing problem for those who wish to study this religion in great depth, there is a different side to this apparent problem. This side is a positive one because the sheer complexity of Hindu teachings means it is also one of the most accessible religions. Whatever form of spiritual or philosophical advancement you want to pursue, the chances are that there will be a certain school of thought within Hinduism that you can get involved with to achieve your goals.

If you decide to convert to Hinduism, it's recommended that you stick to a specific type or form, so you won't get confused. This is because there are various sects within Hinduism. The most popular groups in the West are the Vaishnavites, such as the group established by Swami Prabhupada, the International Society of Krishna Consciousness (ISKCON). The West also welcomed groups, such as the Transcendental Meditation and Yoga groups.

Some of the common sects are:

Vaishnavites — follow Lord Vishnu, or one of his incarnations, as the Supreme Being (exemplified by ISKCON). These incarnations are otherwise referred to as "avatars", the most revered of which are Rama, Narayana, Krishna, and Vasudeva. Also known as Bhagavatism and Krishnaism, this Hindu sect's existence has been traced all the way back to BCE. The numerous schools of thought and denominations which classify under Vaishnavism span across centuries, including the more modern ones such as the ISKCON as well. Within the Vaishnavite sect, the most prominent scriptures are the Upanishads, the Vedas, and the Bhagavad Gita among others.

Shaivites — follow Lord Shiva as the Supreme Being (like the Saiva Siddhanta Church in California). The reverence of this god is expressed through worship within temples and through forms of yoga by Shaivites. Walks of purification, which may lead a devout Shaivite on a journey throughout India, are a known ritual within this sect. Lord Shiva is held as an omnipresent god that dwells in all that is, including the worshippers themselves. Shiva is also regarded as the creator as well as the destroyer, the keeper of everything, and the revealer and concealer of all the truths in life. The rituals undertaken in temples and through yoga have for one of their goals the connection with Shiva within the practicing Shaivite.

Vedics — follow the scriptures from the Upanishadas and Vedas only (embodied famously by the Ramakrishna Mission). The Ramakrishna Mission is part of a global religious organization called the Ramakrishna Movement. With their conduct heavily rooted in the concepts of Karma Yoga, the Ramakrishna Mission focuses on humanitarian work worldwide with rural communities, education, disaster zones, and health. The mission was founded in 1897 and draws teaching from the old philosophies found in the Vedas, more precisely the philosophy of Vedanta.

Shaktites — follow the Goddess Devi as the Supreme Being. Also called Shakti, this god is known as the Divine Mother. While Shakti is the absolute Supreme Being, other divine beings are regarded as her manifestations, of which there are many. As opposed to Shaivism, to which it bears some fundamental resemblance, Shaktism holds the feminine manifestation of divinity, which is Shakti, in the highest regard and almost exclusively worships her. This devotion is also exemplified by the sect's name itself, which translates as the Doctrine of the Goddess in Sanskrit.

Smartism — or the Smarta tradition is another prominent sect within Hinduism. What makes this particular denomination stand out is the fact that five gods are worshiped equally, and those are Vishnu, Ganesha, Shiva, Surya, and Devi or Shakti. The practice itself is closely tied to the Puranas and the many writings, myths, and legends contained within the genre. The Brahmins that focus their studies on the numerous scriptures within the Smriti writings also fall under the category of the Smarta tradition. The origin of the Sanskrit word "Smarta" itself is found in "Smriti."

Meditational/Philosophical Hinduism — follow basic tenets of Hindu religious principles under tutelage of philosophical teachers, and recognize inherent divinity of humanity instead of revolving worship around deities (famously espoused by the Sathya Sai Seva organization or the International Sai Organization in US and Canada).

As the world evolves, the practice of Hinduism is modified based on a person's environment, preferred beliefs, cultural influences, and core path of dedication to deities. The most popular group of deities is the trinity of Brahman, Vishnu, and Shiva, believed to be the creator, preserver and destroyer respectively.

Hindu beliefs can be presented in another way, through the purposes of a Hindu's life:

1. **Dharma** (duties, responsibilities, code of ethics, etc.) — Hindus are bound to fulfill their duties and follow appropriate virtues in their lives, such as honesty, cleanliness, love for peace, penance, austerity, and prayers. There is no direct, one-word translation for the term, but it refers to the laws, rules, and the very order of the universe. The idea of dharma is found in other religions besides Hinduism, such as Buddhism, Jainism, and Sikhism. This set of rules and directions is considered as the highest priority of life in these philosophies. A Hindu must devote his life to adhere strictly to the principles of dharma. Apart from what I already mentioned, dharma also includes rights, virtues, and instructions on the "right way to live." Ultimately, dharma is regarded as divine, cosmic law and its guidelines ensure a life that subscribes to "Rta," which represents the order of the universe, or "truth." References to Rta go back to the times of the old Vedic religion.

2. **Samsara** (universe) — A person is reborn over and over again in the mortal universe, and will live his life according to his Karma. Translated from Sanskrit as "world" or "wandering," Samsara represents a cycle in which one's atman (soul) is

23

incarnated over and over again through multiple lifetimes. It can also be viewed as the reality of mortal existence as a whole. In many Hindu philosophies (as well as in Buddhism and Jainism), Samsara is a mandatory process that every soul must go through before reaching liberation, which is called Moksha and is the ultimate goal of existence. The term is closely tied to the concept of Karma, as the liberation from Samsara only occurs after a soul's Karma has been perfected.

3. **Karma** (right action) — A person gets what he deserves based on his past actions, but may rectify his karmic balance through good deeds in the current life in order to improve his future. Translated from Sanskrit as "world" or "wandering," Samsara represents a cycle in which one's atman (soul) is incarnated over and over again through multiple lifetimes. It can also be viewed as the reality of mortal existence as a whole. In many Hindu philosophies (as well as in Buddhism and Jainism), Samsara is a mandatory process that every soul must go through before reaching liberation, which is called Moksha and is the ultimate goal of existence. The term is closely tied to the concept of Karma, as the liberation from Samsara only occurs after a soul's Karma has been perfected.

4. **Moksha** (liberation) — A person's soul achieves perfection and is liberated from Samsara. This can mean one of two things, depending on the specific school of thought in Hinduism. Widely, it is believed that Moksha liberates the soul itself from worldly hardships and the cycle of Samsara, letting it go on to fulfill its true purpose and reunite with the Supreme Self, the Supreme Soul, or Being – the universe in a sense – as opposed to just being reincarnated again in mortal form. Other philosophies maintain that Moksha simply means a higher level of understanding and self-realization in the course of the current life. This means gaining a full understanding of one's self and soul, thus achieving harmony and a state of total inner peace.

These are the basic beliefs of Hinduism. This is but a bird's eye view of what constitutes Hinduism. The complex and subtle nuances of further teachings will make up part of your studies when you go on to read the Bhagavad Gita and the Vedas.

Chapter 2: Hindu Festivals and Holidays

Just like any other religion, Hinduism has festivals and holidays. Not all Hindus in different parts of the globe get to celebrate these holidays though. But it will help you understand more about Hinduism if you are familiar with these important days.

There are many festivals that are very important to the Hindu religion, some of which are held only as part of various local traditions throughout India and the world. On the other hand, there are numerous festivals which span across all sects and denominations of Hinduism; these make up the pan-Hindu festivals. The dates of these festivals are set in accordance with the lunisolar calendar, with most of them occurring with the arrival of Holi or Diwali, which represent the full moon and the new moon.

<u>**Here are the major Hindu festivals:**</u>

1. Diwali — The Festival of Lights

This is a major holiday for Hindus. It's also known as Divali or Deepavali. During this day, Hindus light diyas (clay lamps) to signify that the light inside their souls has triumphed over the spiritual darkness. People wear new clothes, decorate their homes with lights, and fireworks are lit to celebrate the festival. Hindus also give gifts and prepare delectable sweets or desserts.

Hindus offer prayers to Lakshmi, the Goddess of Wealth. The celebration lasts up to 5 days, for those who strictly follow the holiday. Based on the Hindi Luni-Solar calendar, it starts on the 13th day of Ashwin and ends on the 2nd day of Kartika. This typically falls between October 17 and November 15. To Hindus, it's the equivalent of a New Year's celebration.

There is a general consensus that this is the biggest and most important Hindu festival in the world. Officially, Diwali is recognized as an established holiday in numerous countries, including India, Pakistan, Fiji, Guyana, Malaysia, Singapore, Sri Lanka, and quite a few others. The light decorations that are undertaken during the festivities include millions upon millions of lights, not just at the homes of the worshipers, but also in temples and public buildings.

In preparation, homes and places of work are thoroughly cleaned and brought into perfect order, and then they are decorated. On the night of Diwali, after putting on fresh and new clothes, lamps and candles (referred to as diyas) are lit inside and around the homes of the Hindus. At this time, family prayers called "puja" are initiated in reverence of Lakshmi. Apart from being viewed as the goddess of wealth and prosperity, she is also the goddess of fertility. After the prayers are complete, fireworks are fired to precede the family feasts and the exchanges of gifts among families and circles of friends.

Each of the days during the festival has a name, which may vary according to different denominations and local traditions. In most parts of India, for example, the days are as follows: Dhanteras or the first day of the festivities, then Naraka Chaturdasi, Deepavali, Diwali Padva, and Bhau-beej. The last two days, in the order I laid

29

out, celebrate the sacred bond between wife and husband and that of brother and sister.

An interesting comparison can be made between Diwali and Christmas in the western world. Namely, this Hindu festival is also known as a time of increased shopping and consumerism. During the days of the celebrations, purchases of various items and products drastically increase. Hindus go out to buy many gifts, clothes, jewelry, etc. Unlike in the Christian traditions, though, the shopping is directly encouraged by the faith as Lakshmi is the goddess of wealth, which makes purchases desirable during this time. Smaller festive necessities are also sold in boatloads, such as various candy and pyrotechnic products.

The exact dates for the Diwali based on the Hindu Luni-Solar calendar are the following:

- October 22, 2014, Wednesday

- November 11, 2015, Wednesday

- October 30, 2016, Sunday

- October 19, 2017, Thursday

- November 7, 2018, Wednesday

- October 27, 2019, Sunday

- November 14, 2020, Saturday

2. Holi — The Festival of Colors

Also known as Phagwa or Holaka, Holi is celebrated during Phalguna (early March). Hence, it can denote the end of winter and the start of summer. It's generally a fun day, where Hindus celebrate with parties, dances, colors, balloons, water guns, and eating sweets.

The spring festival of Holi is also seen as the festival of sharing love. This is a festival that lasts for two days in total. Phalguna, the month when the celebrations are undertaken, is defined in the Bikram Sambat Calendar of Hinduism, with the day of the festival being the Purnima or the day of the Full Moon.

While Holi is an old Hindu celebration primarily occurring in India and Nepal, it has spread to non-Hindu communities in South Asia over time.

The festival has also become popular in other parts of the world as well. As a matter of fact, Holi is present in regions of Europe and North America in a similar form, with an emphasis on colors, fun, and love.

The night prior to the festival is when the celebration officially begins with a gathering around a Holika fire, where prayers and other rituals are conducted. The next and main day is called Rangwali Holi, Dhulandi, Dhuleti or Dhulivandan. The day begins early in the morning with a collective color "fight" where many people, from all classes of social standing alike, engage in the playful act of coloring each other with colored water and powders. Using balloons, water guns, and other means of getting the better of their target, whether it is someone they know or not.

This sort of fun can happen in many public places; designated areas around temples as well as parks or simply streets. Food and drinks are usually shared with friends and others as well, with alcohol and other intoxicating drinks being present too, depending on the local customs. As the day approaches its end and the celebrations subside, those who participated proceed to change clothes and make themselves more presentable, before going to visit with loved ones and friends for the evening.

As part of the prayers that occur the night before, a great emphasis is put on fighting the evil within each person. This is a recurring theme of the festival. The festivities are aimed at lighting up the mood, letting people have fun, and most importantly, trying to make amends and connect even with their foes and people who may have wronged them in the past. It is about sharing in the fun with everybody, including those with whom a person may have a strained or broken relationship. The spring festival of Holi is a time to rejoice and forgive for Hindus and others who mark the date.

3. Mahashivaratri — The Great Festival of Shiva

It's also called Shiva Ratri, Maha Shivratri, or The Great Night of Shiva, Understandably, Shaivites consider this an important day because it's Shiva's festival. The day falls on the 14th day of Phalguna, the lunar month. On this day, Hindus pray and sing praises to Lord Shiva. They also offer food believing that Lord Shiva will bring good luck into their lives.

The celebration of Maha Shivaratri consists of two main parts; the first part occurs during the day and the second one during the following night. Before nighttime, the whole day is spent in fasting and chanting of "Om Namah Shivaya," which is Shiva's mantra. The daylight is followed by a vigil that goes on through the night, with rituals of worship that originate in the Vedas. The nightly vigil is called Jaagaran. The significance of the worship being conducted during the night is in that Shiva is believed to be the one who delivers the universe from darkness – meaning ignorance primarily.

At the dawn of the day of the festival, Hindus head to the local Shiva temples first where they engage in Puja, the traditional form of worship. What follows as the sun begins to rise is the ritual of purification in the form of bathing in a designated body of holy water, usually a river such as the Ganges. It's only after the purification process has been completed that the worshippers head back to the temples to prepare the rest of the rituals.

The primary goal of the festivities is gaining good favors with the Lord Shiva through reverence and rituals, as well as commitment via various offerings.

4. Rath Yatra — The Festival of Chariots

This is a day in which the three great chariots with the three deities are paraded in front of believers. This is done in Puri, India and is attended by thousands of devotees from all over India and the world. The three deities honored on this day are: Baladev, the brother of Krishna; Jagannath, the Lord of the Universe, and Subhadra, the sister of Krishna. People dance and feast to celebrate this day.

One of the central rituals amid this festival is the so-called Chera Pahara, which is conducted on the first and the last day of the festival. As part of the ritual, the path before and around the chariots is swept and cleansed by the "Gajapati King" as they proceed to and from the Mausi Maa Temple, on the respective days. A broom with a golden handle and sandalwood water are used for the cleaning. The Gajapati King is to carry out his duties towards the gods with enthusiasm and devotion, despite his power and influence in the Kalinga kingdom. The significance of this ritual is to show that all are equal under Jagannath's divinity, the King and the common followers alike.

Apart from the festival in Puri, where it originated from, there are also the Ratha Yatra of Mahesh and the Dhamrai Ratha Yatra. In many parts of the world, specifically in the west, the festivities are also referred to as the Car Festival and the Chariot Festival. The name Ratha Yatra itself comes from "ratha", which means "chariot," and "jatra," which means "journey," in the Odia language.

5. Janmastami — The Birth of Lord Krishna

Also called Krishna Jayanti or Krishna Janmashtami. This is a big day for Krishna followers because it's a day to celebrate the joy of Krishna's birth. People celebrate the day with dances, music, and drama until midnight. Afterwards, a spiritual service is conducted and then a sumptuous vegetarian feast is enjoyed by all. It's similar to the Christian's celebration of Jesus Christ's birthday (Christmas). Krishna followers offer gifts and prayers to Lord Krishna. You can also decorate your homes with Krishna items to enhance the celebration. This is celebrated on September 15, for the year 2015.

According to the Hindu calendar, the celebration falls on the Krishna Paksha's eighth day, called Ashtami, during the month of Bhadrapad. The dramas that are organized during the holiday contain portrayals of Krishna's life among other things, and these are the most common in Mathura and Vrindavan, as well as other regions where Vaishnavism is prevalent, notably in Manipur. The enactments range from depicting Krishna's days of youth to various sides of her personality and temperament. Under the Gregorian calendar, the day of the celebration for 2016 falls on August 25.

6. Rama Navami—The Chaitra Masa Suklapaksha Navami

This is the celebration of the birthday of Lord Rama, usually in April and March. In 2015, it was on March 15. It's a 10-day celebration characterized by Vedic chanting of mantras in temples. Prayers, flowers, and fruits are offered to Lord Rama too, while some followers would fast throughout the day, and then feast in the evenings.

While Krishna is the eight avatar of Lord Vishnu, Rama is the seventh. During the Chaitra Hindu month, the actual day of Rama's birth comes around on the ninth day of the month, called Navami day. This day comes at the end of the Chaitra-Navaratri celebrations, which go on for nine days. Seeing as Rama is among the oldest Vishnu avatars, Rama Navami is one of the most important festivals in Hinduism.

The chants, recitals, and rituals that are held during the festival are organized in a way that has them increase in intensity towards the holy day of Rama's birth. Another tradition is to have pictures of Rama represented as he was in his infancy, with those images being put into cradles. A great portion of the Hindus who celebrate the festival will engage in fasting during this day, with subsequent feasts in the evening hours, many of which are organized as part of the community.

Here are other Hindu holidays and festivals:

1. Ganesha-Chaturthi

Also known as Ganesha Utsava, it is the Festival of Ganesh which is celebrated between August and September. Also known as the remover of obstacles, Lord Ganesha is one of the most commonly revered deity across the span of Hinduism. This celebration is marked by prayers, offerings, cultural dances, food, and family get-togethers, and is seen as a way of gaining the favor of this son of Shiva and Parvati.

The festival lasts for ten days, beginning on the fourth day of Shukla Chaturthi (the fourth day of the first fortnight) and ending on the Anant Chaturdashi (fourteenth day) in the month of Bhaadrapada.

The celebrations occur in the privacy of the devotees' homes as well as in public places and places of work. The traditions entail construction of shrines of Ganesha by exhibiting clay images of him in various places. As part of the family celebrations in their homes, followers will display a clay image for both friends and family to gather around in worship. When the celebrations reach their conclusion, all of these clay images and idols are submerged in (preferably) natural water sources and dissolved.

Through the rest of the year, Hindus often start any new phase or opportunity by offering a prayer to Lord Ganesha – whether it be a business venture, new car, house, or absolutely any other new gain or capitalization of an opportunity – and display the depth of their gratitude during this festival.

2. Navaratri

Also known as the Festival of Shakti, and is celebrated in the month of September or October. These nine days form a major celebration of Shakti/Devi worship and mark an auspicious period dedicated to nine forms/energies of the Mother Goddess. This festival is capped by a tenth day called Dussehra or Vijayadashami which celebrates the victory of Lord Rama over the demon king Ravana.

The celebration of Shakti during this particular festival comes in the form of worshipping the Mother or Goddess Durga. While Sharad Navaratri is the most prominent kind of this celebration in India and Nepal, there are five types of Navaratri overall.

To be more precise, the celebration goes on for ten days and nine nights in total, during which the followers revere nine forms of Devi (Shakti). The tenth day of the festival known as Dasera comes twenty days before another major festival we mentioned, Diwali.

The festival of Navaratri falls on Pratipada, which is the first day of the bright fortnight in the Hindu lunar month Ashwin and is an annual celebration.

There are still other Hindu festivals that are celebrated depending to the sect that is followed, such as the Durga Puja, Raksha Bandhan, and winter festivals. It will help you understand if you remember that there are more than a thousand deities worshipped by Hindus, and each of them has days of celebration.

Chapter 3: How to Convert to Hinduism

Most people refer to Hinduism as a culture and not a religion and would say that it is not possible to be converted; instead, one must be born a Hindu. Thus, converting to Hinduism can be a gigantic task, especially if you don't know what exact sect to convert to. The following discussion specifically focuses on how to become a Vaishnava (Vaishnavite), who follows Lord Vishnu as the Supreme Being, together with the avatars of Krishna and Rama. It's one of the most followed Hindu sects in the West and all over the world. Here are specific steps that you can implement to convert to Hinduism, specifically, to Vaishnavism.

Step #1 — Learn the basic doctrines of Hinduism

The controversy surrounding the conversion to and from Hinduism is an issue of the recent centuries, rooted in tradition and some of the most basic principles of the religion, at least according to some. Certain religious figures within Hindu circles will wholeheartedly disagree with accepting converts, as they believe that the very concept of proselytization, and most of the other missionary activities for that matter, is directly opposed to basic Hindu ideas.

Outside of India, however, conversion to Hinduism is hardly unheard of and has occurred for a long time regardless of the controversy. The teachings of Hinduism were spread through trade routes in ancient times by merchants coming out of India. These teachings and philosophies were disseminated throughout Southeast Asia, wherever the merchants would go. This ultimately led to conversions as many people were interested in the religion. There is also evidence going back to BCE that shows that conversions may have occurred with the ancient Greeks as well as others. This evidence is found on the Heliodorus pillar. As far as Islam and Christianity are concerned, converting between these religions and Hinduism has been the object of debate only since the 19th century.

Within some circles of Hinduism that espouse various reforms of the religion, there are religious figures who advocate movements such as Shuddhi, with the aim of "reconverting" Muslims and Christians to Hinduism. These efforts are usually present in those regions where the missionary activities of those two religions saw many Hindus converted to their faiths in the past. And while some denominations and movements still oppose that Hinduism adopts such activity, others argue that Hindu leaders need to change their views on proselytization in order to compete with the highly missionary religions such as Islam and Christianity, thus welcoming new followers.

While the debate is still ongoing in most parts of the countries such as Indonesia and India, there are many sects that have wholly adopted the view that Hinduism, too, should open its gates to those who are interested. Still, in order to convert, the first steps must be taken by the would-be convert. If you happen to possess such affinities, it's important to know that the most crucial steps and actions are up to you.

You have to acquire knowledge about the origins and basic beliefs of the Hindu religion, as a whole. You must learn and understand its general beliefs and practices, whichever Supreme Being you choose to follow. Conversion is not a popular word in Hinduism because there are no recommended steps that deal with conversion. You will have to start your own conversion by reading about these beliefs and then start practicing them.

However, smaller sects and temples in your neighborhoods – which follow different deities – may have varying methods of informal conversion. Approaching the priests in one of these temples (of a deity of your choice) and requesting them to perform a conversion ritual by praying to your chosen deity to accept a ritualistic offering on your behalf may sometimes be enough to convert you to Hinduism under that specific deity. You can bring larger amounts of grain and other vegetarian foodstuffs, offer it under your name to the deity, and then request permission from the priests to distribute said foodstuffs to the less fortunate as a sign of respect and sacrifice for your deity as well.

Step #2 — Select your sect

There are various Hindu sects with their own practices and modifications, so you have to select a specific sect or denomination. One of the modernized sects of Hinduism is Vaishnavism. Vaishnavism focuses on doctrines of Lord Vishnu. He is the Supreme Lord prayed to and followed by every Vaishnava. You may select the Vaishnava group that you're most interested in, but the International Society of Krishna Consciousness (ISKCON), established by Swami Prabhupada is most recommended. This group dedicates their services to Lord Krishna.

ISKCON is also known by the name of Hare Krishna movement and was established in New York City back in 1966. Its aforementioned founder is considered a Guru by the followers and is thus worshiped as such. The faith of this particular sect draws teachings from the Hindu scriptures of Bhagavad Gita and Bhagavata Purana. Hare Krishna, in most respects, stems from certain Vaishnava traditions that originated in India during the 15th century. Namely, Gaudiya Vaishnava is the main source of most of the culture and other aspects of ISKCON. The movement of Gaudiya Vaishnava began getting western converts during the first half of the 20th century.

Ultimately, this set the stage for ISKCON to come about in the sixties, aiming to promote bhakti yoga. Worldwide, ISKCON has grown into a large movement with over 550 centers, which incorporate schools, restaurants, various communities, etc. Although Hare Krishna is one of the most prominent global Hindu movements, it is not the only one operating abroad.

If you live in America, the HAF—Hindu American Foundation (http://www.hafsite.org/)—is another option. The group's intention is to promote human dignity, mutual respect and pluralism of all Hindus around the world. There's no specific sect involved, but it bridges the gap between sects and religions for a better understanding of Hinduism. You can join the group and learn about resolving your sect preferences later on.

The importance of the HAF is also in that the United States of America has a Hindu community of around two million followers, whose interests HAF strives to represent. The organization carries out specific work in the public sphere as well, such as publishing of reports concerning the state of human rights of Hindus in the native grounds of South Asia and beyond. The foundation is also notable for getting involved in the California textbook controversy which occurred in 2005, concerning the accuracy of the curriculum as it dealt with Hindu history.

If you wish to engage in spiritual practices which revolve around Hindu traditions and virtue obtained through philanthropic and volunteer work, you can also approach the International Sai organization (http://us.sathyasai.org/) which has centers through the length and breadth of US. This group promotes yogic and meditative practices, holistic approaches to healthy living, and the pursuit of spirituality by fulfilling one's Dharma through the betterment of mankind at large.

Step #3 — Get in touch with the sect you're interested in

Getting in touch with the group will help you get in tune with the sect's beliefs and practices. For the purpose of being more specific about the steps, let's assume that you have selected Vaishnavism. Hence, you can sign up with the International Society of Krishna Consciousness (ISKCON). You can visit the website at http://www.iskcon.org/. There are numerous resources and activities you can get involved in, such as Bhakti Yoga, meditation and the study of the Sacred Texts.

Step #4 — Undergo initiation

Every Vaishnava goes through a process of initiation, where an aspirant finds a guru (spiritual leader) and becomes a disciple. During the initiation, a disciple is given a specific prayer which he will repetitively recite out loud or silently in his mind. The repetitive chanting of prayers (meditation) to Lord Vishnu, or to any one of his ten incarnations is called Japa. The initiation is not mandatory. However, it is recommended as the disciples learn not only the teachings and practices of the Vaishnava but also the values and knowledge of the spiritual leader they have chosen to serve.

If you prefer not to undergo initiation, you can proceed to Step #5 up to Step #8. However, if you can spare the time, it's best to have a guru, who is competent and knowledgeable in turning you into a devout Hindu. This will make the process quicker.

When it comes to converting to Vaishnavism and undergoing initiation, it is important to note that becoming a Vaishnava can either be a difficult or incredibly simple task, depending on how you look at it and what you wish to get out of it. What I mean by this is that, as I've stated before, this religion is more of a way of life than anything else. There is no universally accepted process of conversion and creed in Hinduism. Everyone who adheres to certain principles found in the teachings is a de-facto Hindu, without any official proclamation or marking.

However, to be able to call yourself a Vaishnava and really mean it, you will have to put in the effort and study the philosophy. This is why it may be best to seek assistance on your spiritual undertaking, as gurus and priests will help you get on the path to learning and make the process easier and more organized for you. What makes a Hindu is wisdom and commitment above all, and in the end, this is something you attain wholly on your own. The path to higher knowledge within Hinduism may be long, and this can make the journey hard, but the lack of an established system of conversion is sometimes exactly that which makes Hinduism one of the easier religions to convert to.

Step#5 — Practice Bhakti Yoga

Practicing Bhakti Yoga can be easy with the help of a competent Yoga teacher, but with some practice, you can also do it on your own. In Bhakti Yoga, you connect to the Supreme Being through your acts. There are other types as well, such as Jnana Yoga, Hatha Yoga, and Karma Yoga.

This form of yoga is widely regarded among Hindus as the easiest and simplest road an everyday person can take towards spiritual balance and development. The reason that Bhakti Yoga is so accessible is that it does not require a full-time commitment as the practice itself is not as strict as some of the other forms of yoga.

The Bhakti movement is a crucial movement within Hinduism, which originated during the medieval era, as a response to the spread of Islam and the subsequent conflicts between Hinduism and Muslims, as some experts state. The Bhakti movement saw the most rapid spread between the 15th and 17th centuries. Vaishnavism, Shaktism, and Shaivism all fall under the wing of the Bhakti movement.

The Upanishads are especially important for the Bhakti school of thought, most notably the Shvetashvatara Upanishad. The wisdom and teachings of Bhakti Yoga can be well-understood from the Bhagavad Gita and the Purana literature.

Essentially, Bhakti Yoga is seen as a means of getting in touch with one's love and reverence of God and expressing that deep-seated love through the practice. The teachings of Bhakti Yoga refer to a kind of love for God that is unconditional and is in its purest form. This means that a devotee will exercise the Yoga exclusively with the aim to please the Supreme Being, without expecting any form of reward whatsoever.

In Sanskrit, Bakhti translates as a certain state of mind or, more precisely, an attitude that is characterized by a firm devotion to God on a personal level. In a slightly different explanation, this devotion is on the level of one's soul. Thus, it is really a relationship between the soul of God (the Hindu idea of the Supreme Soul or Self) and that of the individual worshiper.

In the Purana literature, nine forms of Bhakti are outlined. Those include Sravana, Kirtan, Visnoh Smarana, Vandana, Dasya, Pada Sevana, Arcana, Sakhya, and Atma Nivedana.

The meaning of these yogi practices as part of Bhakti and other forms of meditation or yoga is as follows:

- Sravana refers to reading or listening to the stories of Krishna, found in various scriptures such as the Hindu epics.

- Kirtan is the practice of chanting and musical expression during rituals of yoga or meditation. It also denotes collective singing as part of worship.

- Visnoh Smarana is simply an act of mindfulness where the practitioner of yoga focuses all of his thoughts on Lord Vishnu.

- Giving homage and respect to a deity is done through Vandana, while Dasya represents servitude.

- Pada Sevana means rendering service, while Arcana, Sakhya, and Atma Nivedana represent the worshiping of a deity's image, friendship, and surrendering of the self to the Supreme, respectively.

These form the key principles to be followed as a Hindu proceeds to worship and show devotion to God through Bhakti practices.

Step #6 — Practice meditation

The meditation techniques for Vaishnavas or Vaishnavites can be complex. It combines mantras, names of God and Sanskrit syllables with the yoga process. The Maha Mantra, which is the great mantra for deliverance is recited, making use of three words: Hare, Krishna, and Rama. It has been observed that people who perform the meditation not only experienced happiness, peace, and strength, but also maintained good health. It is also meant to establish a close relationship with the Supreme Being, while eliminating selfish emotions, such as greed, jealousy, anger, bitterness, and envy.

Aside from being paramount to most, if not all, Hindu practices, meditation has been a vital aspect of many other religions since ancient times. More importantly for the modern world and the contemporary times, meditation finds much use in everyday life throughout the world. It doesn't take a very thorough look at the popular culture, even in the west, to realize that numerous forms of meditation and yoga have found their place in the developed world as either a way to decompress and relax or a form of therapy in many regards.

You can use the three methods below:

- **Japa Mala** — You recite God's name using 108 Rosary beads to help you concentrate. Primarily, the term Japa Mala refers to the string of beads itself, used as part of Japa. The recital can be done quietly out loud, or it can stay in the mind as you engage. The main purpose of the beads while used for concentration is to count the repetitions of your recital. Seeing as Japa meditation can be done in a meditative posture (sitting down) or while you're up and about on your feet, the bead string is useful in that it can be hung around your neck and thus kept close regardless of what form of meditation you're practicing.

- **Kirtan** — You sing God's names with musical instruments. This can be complex to persons who are not used to it. But if you're interested in this method, you will certainly gain the expertise through constant practice.

Kirtan originates from old Vedic traditions, and it represents a whole spectrum of religious performances that incorporate musical performances, primarily as part of a narration. This is also exhibited in the original Sanskrit meaning of the word, which is "narrating," "telling" or "describing" something.

Kirtan is found in other religions such as Buddhism or Sikhism as well. In Hinduism, particularly, Kirtan is another tradition spread far and wide by the Bhakti movement during the middle ages among the followers of Vaishnavism and Shaivism. Records of the Kirtan traditions are also found in the Bhagavad Gita.

- **Sankirtan**—When you perform the Kirtan with a group, it's called Sankirtan. This is believed to be powerful because the spiritual strength comes from a number of individuals.

Steps in performing Maha Mantra meditation (This can also serve as your yoga):

1. **Find a quiet, safe and less illuminated place.** This can be in your room or anywhere inside your house.

For any form of meditation to produce results, it is paramount that you eliminate any and all distractions in your environment and immediate surroundings. This means getting the lights down to a volume that won't affect your eyes at all to start with, as having to squint your eyes or having a light source shining too brightly in your visual field are disturbances that may interfere with your level of focus.

Although environmental noises can be a distraction, this generally means television, traffic, and other loud and disturbing sounds. However, certain sounds can actually improve ambiance in some form of meditation, so keep that in mind. These are continuous, quiet, soothing sounds such as the humming of a fridge or blowing from a fan. Such noises can relax the mind and bolster concentration.

2. **Do the yoga pose.** Sit cross-legged on the floor, with your back straight and your hips elevated above your knees. You can use pillows to elevate your hips to the desired position.

This is a well-known position in countless forms of yoga and meditation practice that the vast majority of people are familiar with. It offers good balance and ensures that your body is not strained in any way. Being in a position that stresses your muscles or wearing uncomfortable clothes that press onto you are also distractions that make meditation difficult. It's important to bring all physical sensations down to a minimum.

3. **Put your palms together.** Start with the bases of the palms, then the palms, and then the fingers.

Allow the energy to flow between your palms by leaving a small space in between them.

4. **Slightly bow your head towards your chest.** This should bring your chin towards your chest.

5. **Set your goal in doing the meditation.** What do you want to achieve? It should be specific and clear. But it can also be simple, such as to relax.

Meditation works much better when you have an objective in mind, especially if it's an abstract or spiritual goal. This is why the practice is so popular in religious circles. If you are using an object or mantra to strengthen your focus, the main goal of your exercise should rest in the back of your head at all times. However, a goal such as relaxation, worship of a deity, getting in touch with your spirit, or relieving a pain you may be suffering from, can all serve as an object to focus on just the same.

6. **Allow your hands to rest on your thighs.**

7. **Observe how you inhale and exhale air**. But DON'T control your breathing.

The trick is to differentiate between diaphragmatic (abdominal) and chest breathing. For the purposes of meditation, breathing by moving your belly is more desirable for a couple of reasons. Most importantly, by breathing in this manner, the oxygen you take in is distributed through your blood much more effectively, which means that more of it reaches your brain, thus improving the calming effects of meditation. Efficient breathing is otherwise known as a great way to help with anxiety attacks and stress, outside of just meditation.

However, if you are a chest breather like many adult human beings are, it might take a conscious effort on your part to switch to belly breathing. This effort will, naturally, make you aware that you are breathing, and as you try to switch your method, you are likely to end up breathing manually – controlling your breathing. This is a common problem for those who are new to meditation. If at first you don't succeed, that's alright too, because you will gradually adopt belly breathing as your default, until it becomes an effortless habit.

The simple task of observing your breathing without controlling it may prove troublesome for many people as well. This is also a matter of practice and focus. Keep trying and you will eventually learn to be a mere observer of your bodily functions, able to count your breaths while they are still occurring automatically. When you reach this stage, you will have made significant progress in your meditation practice.

Assuming the right positions, which are specified as part of most meditations' doctrines, helps you breathe more easily too. There has to be as little pressure on your chest and abdomen as possible, which means always keeping a straight back, among other things. Eventually, your breathing will become more efficient and easy in everyday life as well, and adopting belly breathing has been scientifically proven to have many health benefits.

8. **Chant the mantra you selected.** You can chant it loudly or mentally. It's up to you. The purpose of the mantra is to induce a more relaxed state

and to enhance your meditation. You can use the three-word mantra, "Hare Krishna; Hare Rama", or create a combination of the words that you find most effective. Continue with this step until you achieve your goal.

An example of a mantra is this:

Hare Krishna, Hare Krishna

Krishna, Krishna, Hare Hare

Hare Rama, Hare Rama

Rama Rama, Hare Hare

This is the Maha Mantra itself, otherwise known as the Hare Krishna mantra. The mantra is widespread throughout Vaishnavism and is recorded in the Upanishad of Kali Santarana. The sixteen words that make up this chant refer to the avatars Hare, Rama, and Krishna. While the mantra became increasingly popular thanks to the Bhakti movement during the 15th century, the ISKCON movement spread the famous chant throughout the world, well beyond its original grounds.

9. **Shift to silent meditation.** After chanting the mantra until you've achieved your desired state, you can now stay silent and just focus on your inhalation and exhalation. Stay this way as long as you want. This will allow you to achieve greater heights of meditation and relaxation.

10. **You can repeat these steps as often as you want.** It takes constant practice to obtain your desired results but don't give up. Meditation is a skill, and just like any other skill, it needs practice.

Make no mistake, a meditative state is an actual state of consciousness and not merely the act of sitting and feeling rested. Through perseverance, this skill can be mastered by anybody, and once you manage to achieve this specific state, you will begin to see what it actually means. Meditation has been used since ancient times not only to relax an individual but to induce a trance-like state where one can begin to observe his own consciousness from a separate perspective, so to speak.

This practice can offer an individual deep insight into their mind. Thus, meditation is really a form of increased control over one's own thoughts and feelings. It may prove more difficult to achieve than you may think at first, but it is well worth the effort to gain more control over yourself and thus learn to channel negative feelings as you see fit. This is only scratching the surface of what trained and erudite individuals can and have achieved through meditation for centuries.

Step #7 — Become a lacto-vegetarian

This is an important step since lacto-vegetarianism is emphasized upon in Vaishnavism. If you're carnivorous, you have no other option but to let go of this eating habit. So, think hard before converting. Once you're committed to becoming a Vaishnavite, you have to stop eating meat, fish, and eggs altogether. Your food should comprise of Ahimsa milk (milk obtained through non-violent methods) and vegetables. Vaishnavites believe that even when choosing food, they should show compassion and mercy. Hence, they avoid foods that come from killing living things.

Another option is to prepare your own lacto-vegetarian food; there are numerous Vaishnava vegetarian cook books online and offline that you can refer to. If you don't have the luxury of time to read and cook, you can simply buy food from the vegetarian Hindu food outlet in your area. Also, the ISKCON group usually holds vegetarian cooking classes in Hindu temples, and you can oft to join one of these classes. In addition, ISKCON also has the Food for Life Program that distributes daily sanctified vegetarian food to members who are in need of it. That's why it's important that you join a group if you want to benefit from the help they have to offer.

If nothing else works better for you, then you can simply boil your veggies to ascertain that you don't eat any of the prohibited foods. Furthermore, you should also prepare your food properly by having the correct attitude when you cook—that of compassion and love. For Vaishnavas, even the preparation of food is a spiritual experience. You should cook your food when you're free of hatred, greed and sinful emotions.

However, if you do not wish to convert to vegetarianism, it would be recommended that you consider practicing other forms of Hinduism by approaching temples in your localities, rather than joining sectarian organizations – those often being vegetarian by nature. Though most of these larger organizations may shun meat, Hinduism in itself does not promote vegetarianism across the board – only the complete shunning of beef in one's diet, and observing vegetarianism on select high holidays and periods of prayer. In fact, even among religio-cultural Hinduism, those who take the oaths of priests (Brahmans) or follow other Hindu groups like Jainism form a majority of compulsive vegetarians.

Step #8—Study the Sacred Texts of the Bhagavad Gita and the Vedas

The Sacred Texts of the Bhagavad Gita is considered the ultimate source of spiritual wisdom for Hindus. It's a Hindu scripture composed of the conversation between Arjuna, the warrior, and Lord Krishna. The event occurred before the Mahabharata War, an epic war in ancient India. This has been translated to an enlightening, spiritual context by Swami Prabhupada, and has often enriched and guided Hindus towards their spiritual fulfillment.

In the Gita, Arjuna refused to go to war because he feared that he may inflict pain or injury upon his kinsmen, friends, and teachers, whereupon Lord Krishna explained to Arjuna his duties as a warrior. Their discourse demonstrated the concepts of a relationship with God, the liberation of the soul, and the yoga tenets of devotion (Bhakti Yoga), non-attached action (Karma Yoga), and knowledge (Gyana

Yoga). You have to study these sacred texts if you want to become a Vaishnavite.

You have to study the Vedas (knowledge) too. This will play a significant role as a source of your spiritual nourishment. There are four Vedas, the Rigveda, the Atharvaveda, the Samaveda and the Yajurveda. These Vedas disclose information about almost anything of value; from medicine to ethics, to meditation and many varied and important concerns in life. This is done through a collection of poems, hymns, prayers, formulas, and texts. You can learn how a Vaishnava must behave in given situations. The study of holistic medicine (Ayurveda) is also included.

The Hindu texts have been successfully translated into more than 70 languages. You can access the summary of each chapter of the Bhagavad Gita from the ISKCON website through its book distribution section for free. If you prefer to own an English translation of the Bhagavad Gita and the Vedas, you can also buy the complete translation from Amazon.com. If you don't have time to read, an audio of the book is also available in Hindi and English at Amazon.com.

Step #9—Live the life of a Vaishnava

To be a Vaishnava, one must embrace the life of a Vaishnava, initiated or not. Vaishnavites believe that Lord Vishnu is the Supreme God. Therefore, you have to live just as Lord Vishnu wants you to live. With the help of a group or an organization, you can do this more easily because there are programs that can help you fulfill your role as a Vaishnava.

Depending on where you are located and which sects or organizations operate there, it's possible that you can do volunteer work with them and get closer to the community in this way. ISKCON, for example, is known as an organization that does all sorts of humanitarian work wherever the need may arise. Hare Krishna volunteers offer help when disaster strikes; they help out in the fields of education and healthcare, and they conduct small-time volunteer work as well. You can help distribute things such as food or books, assist in administration, work around temples, lend a hand in various kitchens and the organization of festivals, etc.

More importantly than just participating with the sect you're interested in, volunteering is always a good way to do something significant, something you can be proud of. You can refer to the ISKCON website for further details, especially if you are in London.

These are the recommended steps you can take if you want to convert to Hinduism, specifically Vaishnavism. You can modify the steps to suit your preferences. It's necessary to take note of the important aspects of reincarnation, yoga, meditation and Karma.

Chapter 4: Basic Hindu Rituals

Hinduism around the world is made up of compounded blends of specifically Hindu beliefs and the previous religious beliefs (if any) of the person. There are 16 Hindu Samskaras (sacraments or rituals) which follow the life of a believer from birth to death. Although not all Hindus observe these rituals, you should at least be familiar with them.

1. **Garbhadhana** — This involves the chanting of mantras and the placing of the hands on the bride's forehead to purify her and her husband so that the bride can conceive a healthy and pure fetus. This is done immediately after the marriage.

   Garbhadhana is known as the ritual to commemorate a couple's intent and will to have a child. Otherwise called Garbhalambhanam, the Sanskrit word translates to "attaining the wealth of the womb." In some of the older records, this term is ascribed simply to the act of fornication within the married couple as they proceed to conceive a child, without reference to any sort of formal ceremony.

The ritual is said by certain scholars to originate from Vedic hymns, contained in Rigveda, for example. In modern times, Garbhadhana is undertaken as a private ceremony for a newly married couple.

2. **Pumsavana** — This is done in the third month of pregnancy to ensure that the fetus grows healthily.

"Quickening the fetus rite," or Pumsavana, is a rite of passage that stems from the Atharva Veda, wherein sections of the text cite recitations that are to be used to bolster the growth of a male fetus, while other sections exist that offer the same for both genders.

The third month of pregnancy is especially meaningful due to the fact that the baby usually begins to move and kick inside the womb at this time, which is seen as a crucial step in the child's development.

Just like most of the other rituals and traditions in the Hindu religion, this rite of passage varies from one location to the next, but all of the practices overlap in some basic respects. For example, this common ground is the rule that the husband is to serve a specially prepared meal to the wife as part of his role in the process.

3. **Simantonnayana** — This is done in the fourth or fifth month of pregnancy to ensure that the mother overcomes whatever emotional problems she may have, and to eradicate negative feelings that may endanger both mother and child.

The most elemental aspect of this rite of passage, which is generally observed wherever the ritual takes place, is the idea of friends and family gathering with the expecting couple. The pregnant woman is to be given gifts, according to many traditions, allowed to rest and encouraged to relax and avoid stress. This stage is when increasing efforts are being made to accommodate and please the woman that is expecting.

4. **Jatakarman** — This is done after the birth of a male child to ascertain and enhance the child's normal development and growth.

Translated from Sanskrit as "the rite of a newborn infant", the ritual is written down in the Brihadaranyaka Upanishad. Apart from celebrating the birth of the child, the rite is significant in that it commemorates the bond between the newborn and the father. Generally, the tradition has the father use honey and ghee to touch with them the lips of his infant child. All the while, hymns from the Vedas are being recited to wish the child a welcome to the world and a long life to follow.

5. **Namakarana**—This ceremony is done on the 12th day after birth. Its purpose is to name the child. Prayers are offered to seek blessings for the child.

The purpose of the ritual is also its translation from Sanskrit. Before the chosen name is announced by the child's parents, the baby is washed and freshly dressed earlier on the day of the ritual. The key significance of this rite of passage is in that it formally marks the child as a person and an individual in the world, to be accepted as such by people in his life.

The ritual is continued with the parents gathering their friends and family members, who are to bring gifts to the parents and indulge in feasting together.

6. **Nishkramana** — This is done when a child is first taken out of the house to see the external environment. The parents must show the sun, the moon and the stars to the child.

Undertaken during the fourth month after the child's birth, Nishkramana represents a formal way of making the baby acquainted with the world around. The ritual is conducted with both of the parents present for the occasion, as well as other family members and friends if possible and desired. Like during the Namakarana, parents are to bathe and freshly clothe their child for the ritual.

Aside from this approach, some families follow a tradition where their child is brought to their temple of worship for the first time and introduced to the world in that way.

7. **Annaprashana** — This is done in the 6th month, when a child starts to eat. A silver or golden spoon is used in giving his first food.

As it is written in some Hindu texts, the child doesn't necessarily have to be completely denied breastfeeding from that point on. Instead, it is recommended that the process of transitioning to solid food be a gradual one, where the child is fed food more frequently over time, while still being supported by breast milk. The first food that the child is given is usually cooked rice, or a food based on that, as it is soft and ideal to start with. Of course, customs vary, and some traditions will switch their children's diets completely to a solid food right away.

8. **Chudakarana** — This is done when the child's hair is cut for the first time. This typically happens when the child is 3 years old.

With most traditions, the hair cutting includes the shaving of the child's head as well. The ritual is conducted in the presence of both parents, and the child's nails are also cut.

As cleanliness is an important part of the Hindu Dharma, the ritual signifies the child's acceptance of this rule. Depending on local practice, this rite of passage is to be undertaken when the child is around one year of age, with others going over the age of three. Chudakarana may also include recitations to wish good fortune and health upon the child, as is the case in the Jatakarman ritual.

9. **Karnavedha** — This is done when the child's ear is pierced and earrings are worn.

This ritual is not universally observed and is instead more of an optional ceremony. Customs around this rite of passage vary, with some traditions stating that it is to be done within a month after the baby's birth or within a year according to others. The piercing itself is done with a silver needle or a golden thread, for boys and girls alike. If the child is a female, her left ear is pierced first, while the opposite is observed for the boys. The significance of the ritual is to introduce the child to the Hindu culture, which is heavily invested in the ornamentation of the body, as well as to consolidate their social participation.

10. **Vidyarambham (Aksharabhyasam)** — This is done when the child starts his education and the child encounters his first alphabet.

During the ritual, the parents, along with relatives who want to help, introduce the child to basic means of acquiring further knowledge. Apart from the alphabet, the young child is also tried with numbers and geometrical shapes as part of an introduction to mathematics. Musical instruments are also part of the ritual at times.

As knowledge is one of the crucial aspects of Hinduism, this form of rite of passage is very important. However, some texts, particularly the old ones, skip the Vidyarambham and proceed straight to the next one, Upanayana, which essentially concerns the same aspect of life.

11. **Upanayana** — This "Thread Ceremony" is conducted so that the child's soul is purified, and he vows to listen to his guru to live a life adhering to the Hindu teachings, without complaints.

This significant ritual marks the "second birth" of a young child as he initiates contact with those who carry knowledge and teach. As part of the ceremony, a guru sets the ritual in motion by introducing the child to knowledge. This rite of passage formally marks the milestone that is the beginning of a child's education. Because of the importance and purpose of the ritual as it pertains to one's spiritual growth, Upanayana has been compared to the ritual of baptism in Christian religions.

In ancient times, this rite of passage was more complex, consisting of many rituals that involved the child and the family. Furthermore, it used to be a ritual specifically designed for children around the age of eight, but it has since become available to people of other ages as well.

12. **Praishartha** — This is a ritual involving the child's learning of the Vedas and Upanishadas. The child commits himself to gaining spiritual knowledge from the Sacred Scriptures.

Otherwise referred to as Vedarambha, this ritual marks another important milestone, which is the very beginning of studying the scripture in school. In most texts, this ceremony involves fire and a sit-down between the teacher and the new

79

student. The process begins with the teacher reciting certain hymns out loud while the student reciprocates.

In some of the older scriptures, this particular ritual is seldom mentioned. It is suggested by some that this ritual came about later as a difference between the formal start of schooling and the actual introduction to the Vedas and Upanishads was acknowledged.

13. **Keshanta and Ritushuddhi** — This is a ritual done for boys and girls respectively, to enrich their spiritual development. These two rituals are essentially coming of age celebrations for both genders.

Keshanta is the male youth's rite of passage. It involves the first shaving of the boy's facial hair. According to most texts, this ritual is to be conducted at age sixteen and involve gift exchanges, recitations, and a vow of chastity on the boy's part.

Ritushuddhi is the coming of age ritual for females. Naturally, it is held after the young girl has had her first menstruation and begins turning into a woman. The ceremony is a gathering of family and friends who present gifts to the girl. She is also given her first half-sari dress, which she is to keep and wear at ceremonies until she is married.

14. **Samavartana** — This is done at the end of the child's formal education. The grown man is now free of his previous vows, and can now follow his life's goal through the help of his guru or religious adviser.

The young man is ceremonially bathed and cleansed, symbolizing that he has been "bathed in knowledge." This rite of passage is usually to occur around the age of twenty-one, after an education of at least twelve years. Traditionally, the ritual would see the students and their teacher gather around for the ceremony, with dharma recitations and fire rituals, after which the bath commences. According to Hindu teachings by large, this milestone does not necessarily mean that the young man is to marry right away, but is instead free to pursue other goals before taking his vows.

15. Vivaha — This is a ritual done during the marriage ceremony, where the couple pledges to be loyal and honest with each other. Mantras are chanted to shower the married couple with blessings. According to Hindu rituals, the bond of marriage does not end with the demise of the partners – but stretches across seven lifetimes on the whole.

The celebrations associated with Vivaha can last for a few days in total as they consist of multiple rituals and rites of passage. Rituals cover the giving away of the daughter by her father, a symbolic seven-step walk with vows being spoken, and the marking of the union by holding hands near the fire. There are some variations across Hinduism, but these are generally the key steps through which most traditions overlap. The wedding ceremony usually entails Vedic hymns as well, since Vivaha is a Vedic ritual originally.

The welcoming of the bride to the groom's home and her acquaintance with the family, the fourth day of the marriage, and the first time the couple shares the bed are also marked in a ritualistic manner.

16. **Antyeshti or Antima Sanskar** — This is done during the time of cremation and acts as the final funeral rites. Although there have been certain sects which have espoused burial practices instead, Hinduism by and large holds that the soul needs to be freed from the presence of its mortal shell if it is to move on. To this end, cremation by fire is carried out to allow the pure soul to leave the impure shell behind in its continuation along the cycle of rebirth, and the ashes are often drifted along running water bodies (rivers, seas, oceans; water bodies where the water doesn't pool and stagnate) which may hold holy significance.

These are the basic rituals of Hindus. There are still more minor rituals that the various sects follow. Since the sect recommended here is Vaishnavism, you can have a clearer understanding of what rituals you should follow once you join the group of your choosing. It doesn't mean though that you have to strictly abide by the rituals. But if rituals are not specified, you can choose the ones you feel comfortable with.

Chapter 5: Hinduism Compared to Other Major Religions

Hinduism does not adhere to a single edict or belief just like Christianity and Islam. As the religion grew with members from all over the world, the basic beliefs were also integrated into the existing lives of Hindus. Unlike Christianity and Islam, Hinduism isn't a monotheistic faith but is actually polytheistic in practice, with Hindus worshiping various deities even if their sects revolve around a singular central god or goddess.

Still, Hinduism is so diverse that almost all forms of worship and concepts of divinity can be found in the many traditions that have developed on their own throughout the centuries. While most of the sects are polytheistic in practice at least, monotheism can be found in some, as well as atheism.

The atheist schools of thought that are found in Hinduism are primarily atheistic in the respect that they reject the concept of God as an explicable, personal entity, while the idea of a creator God is also rejected. Philosophies such as Yoga, Samkhya, and Mimamsa are a few that espouse such beliefs. Atheism is also found with some of the Hindus who view Hinduism strictly as a way to live and thrive spiritually, instead of as a stern and defined religious practice.

The sects that appear polytheistic in practice, on the other hand, are such for a reason. Namely, most of the prominent Hindu denominations focus their worship and reverence on a single Supreme Being whose name is well-known. However, it is found in scripture, notably in Purana literature and the Hindu Epics, that those Gods usually have their avatars. A term I have mentioned a few times before in this book, avatars are merely incarnations of the one, Supreme God, through which God exerts powers for a specific purpose. The avatars of God are divine and worshiped nonetheless, thus giving many Hindu sects an appearance of a polytheistic religion. The most well-known such case is Lord Vishnu, who has numerous avatars that are all equally worshiped, the most prominent of which are Krishna and Rama.

Some common ground between Hinduism and other popular religions, such as Christianity, is also found in the belief that the soul is eternal. Granted, there are major differences as to the position of this soul in the cosmic arena and the way it moves on after the body has died, but the idea is similar on the most fundamental level.

In Christianity, the general idea is that the judgment of a soul and its potential admittance to heaven or banishment to hell is something that's left entirely up to God. If a Christian has done wrong in his life, he can sincerely repent, and it is believed that God is merciful and will forgive one's transgressions if the repentance was true, allowing the soul into heaven. However, the end decision is still that of God, and a mortal individual can take certain steps and merely hope for the best. On the other hand, a Hindu has a dharma and the concepts of Karma. If he adheres to the tenets found here with all his effort, salvation is guaranteed in this life or one of the upcoming ones.

The liberation of one's soul from samsara is not one of the possible outcomes; it is rather the ultimate goal towards which every soul strives. What this means, essentially, is that the worst case scenario for a soul in Hinduism is that it remains in samsara, a cycle it is already in. Life or lives can get harder due to bad Karma, but as far as the spiritual position of a soul in the universe is concerned, either it can remain unchanged, or it can get better when the soul leaves samsara. This is an important difference when comparing Hinduism to Christianity. The concept of hell is a much different idea, as it means that a soul will be doomed to agony and torment for an eternity. The notion of divine punishment is, therefore, much more specific and concrete in Christianity, while Hinduism leans more towards the idea of an individual being the one who writes his destiny, with an infinitely long deadline to change his ways.

To help you understand more about Hinduism, here's a general comparison of Hinduism with the three major religions: Christianity, Judaism, and Islam.

On Reincarnation and Karma

Hinduism believes in reincarnation and Karma just like the other religions in India, such as Buddhism, Jainism and Sikhism. There are slight differences in the beliefs but basically, these religions believe in reincarnation.

On the other hand, Christianity, Judaism, and Islam don't believe in reincarnation. Christianity believes in the concept of hell and heaven; in Judaism, some Jews believe in the afterlife, while some don't; while in Islam, Muslims believe in the resurrection of the body and soul and of hell and heaven afterwards. Since Hinduism believes in a perpetual cycle of rebirth, ending only with salvation and oneness with the Supreme Being, there are few defined concepts of hell. However, there are defined ideas of "purgatory", as seen in some sects and central texts - where suffering souls are held in limbo for periods of time which vary depending on the amount of one's accrued sins in that lifetime, before finally moving on to the next life.

However, the concept of Karma is reflected in the other religions with some passages, such as the Christian passage about the Golden Rule, "Do unto others what you want others do unto you." This denotes that you must treat other people the way you want to be treated. Hence, it reflects Karma—in a sense. In Judaism, the bible of the Jews is the Old Testament of Christians, so there's a relationship of the teachings at this particular level.

There are also other principles found in the Bible that may be interpreted as denoting the concept of Karma to a certain extent. The old phrase "Live by the sword, die by the sword" is a great example of earthly Karma. Although the proverb originated in ancient Greece, it was later found in the Bible where Jesus Christ says to one of his followers, who had just committed an act of violence, "Return thy sword to its place, for all who will take up the sword will die by the sword." This simple wisdom implies a form of Karma that isn't necessarily divine or cosmic, but merely logical and to be expected. Those who use violence as a means to achieve their ends will, ultimately, attract reciprocation not only from those they have wronged but from those who lead a similar life. He who has killed others can surely expect the same fate as violence breeds more thereof.

As can be seen, there is nothing mystical about such concepts of Karma. This bad Karma is acquired by mortal people through mortal deeds, and the consequences are always executed by other mortal humans. The whole circle closes in the course of a single human lifetime, regardless of the Christian notions of hell and heaven in the afterlife. The main difference between these principles and the Hindu concepts of Karma, therefore, becomes apparent. Either way, the idea of the cause and effect with respect to moral or immoral action is the same in essence.

While Christians believe that Jesus Christ is the Son of God, that he forms an aspect of God's divinity through the trinity of the Father, the Son, and the Holy Spirit, and that he died and was resurrected from the dead, Hindus don't believe that. Jews and Muslims, on the other hand, believe that Jesus Christ was a mortal prophet of God and not divine by nature.

All in all, the teachings of other religions have the basic tenets just like Hinduism, such as:

- Don't kill

- Don't steal

- Honor your parents

- Don't covet other people's wives

- Don't bear false witness

It's evident that the core, underlying principles of what is moral and immoral behavior are all but universal. This is a testament to an age-old effort of civilization to curtail wrongdoing and promote virtuous living, at least within a particular society, and control impulses which may sometimes be destructive. Overall, Hinduism is an epitome of a philosophy that strives to make wisdom a way of life. It is, therefore, incredibly complex and diverse and constitutes the world's third largest religion by the number of devotees.

Hindus are still growing in number across the globe. This trend will continue as more people realize that the basic edicts of Hinduism are applicable with ease to their daily lives.

A lot of the appeal of Hinduism comes from the applicability of the most of its principles in daily life. As I've stated before, the philosophy is such that many simply consider it a way of life, but this also makes it possible to pick out rituals, beliefs, and practices that are most suitable for your personal lifestyle. Plus, many Hindu practices are simply useful to us, especially since a lot of them are about inner peace, spiritual balance, and calmness – states that are pursued relentlessly in the modern world so full of stresses.

Hinduism compared to Buddhism

The first and foremost thing that Buddhism and Hinduism share is that they both originate from the Indian subcontinent. Of course, the most prominent differences are found in principles, traditions, and practice. Through many centuries and into the middle ages, Buddhism declined in popularity on the home grounds, but it has gone on to spread through much of Asia. Subsequently, it has become a majority religion in multiple countries, with close to a half of the total Buddhist population of the world living in

China, where they make up around 18% of the country. Although reincarnation, among numerous other beliefs, is a common concept between these two religions, there are still some fundamental differences to be observed. It is also worth noting that Buddhism, much like Hinduism, is not considered a religion by many, but rather a philosophy with many followers.

Buddhism is also a religion that can easily be regarded as a way of life as it is essentially a dharma to be followed by devotees throughout their life. One of the most striking discrepancies, when compared to Hinduism, is the atheistic nature of Buddhism. Namely, Buddhism generally rejects the idea of any one God as a creator or overseer of our universe. Like all the other teachings found in the philosophies of Buddhism, the atheistic outlook was also espoused by the Buddha. In contrast, as you have read, Hinduism is definitely a theistic religion, regardless of how diverse the beliefs may be. Although some schools of thought in Hinduism do embrace atheism, these are by far a minority.

Buddha is mentioned throughout Hindu teachings, but the way Hindus regard him is different in many ways. Some traditions view him simply as a holy man, while others state that he was an incarnation or avatar of Lord Vishnu. Buddhists ascribe no divine aspects to Buddha.

As I've stated, one of the most significant overlaps between these religions is the idea of reincarnation or the continuous cycle of rebirth. However, a difference lays in the concepts of a soul's liberation at the end of the cycle or, more precisely, what this salvation means and how it manifests. This concerns the comparison between moksha and nirvana. Furthermore, in many Hindu traditions, a soul's salvation could only be attained by Brahmins, while in Buddhism, any soul, regardless of positions or caste, could reach nirvana through devotion.

In Buddhism, the ultimate goal of one's life is to reach nirvana. As a follower of the Buddhist path reaches this state, he becomes liberated from the pain of repeated rebirths – Buddhist samsara. The way one achieves the state of nirvana is by adhering to the principles of the Noble Eightfold Path, or the Middle way, which is the Buddha's fourth Noble Truth. The principles found in the Noble Eightfold Path are right view, right speech, right resolve, right livelihood, right conduct, right effort, right mindfulness, and right Samadhi.

The philosophy of nirvana is an old and complex one, which requires a lot of devotion to master. In the simplest terms, this state of mind and spirit marks the peak of one's spiritual growth, the very apex of spirituality. One common and simple enough explanation is found within Buddhist tradition itself. It is said that the achievement of nirvana represents that an individual has managed to extinguish the "three fires" or purge the "three poisons" from their spirit. These three mortal fetters are passion, aversion, and ignorance.

It's worth noting that, much like Hinduism, Buddhism too has its own branches and varying traditions. Some of them may have different views on the goal of one's life and a different idea of salvation from reincarnation. In some schools of thought, the goal of the Buddhist path is not to reach nirvana specifically, but to achieve Buddhahood, rising to the level of spirituality and wisdom comparable to that of the Buddha.

Unlike Hinduism, Buddhism has a well-known and acknowledged founder of the philosophy. Buddha was a Hindu prince who decided to go his own way and form a new direction of teaching and spirituality. Therefore, Buddhism is sometimes seen as a branch that broke off the tree of Hinduism, although the philosophy has since taken different directions in many respects.

On one last note, the two philosophies differ when it comes to gender roles and equality as well. Hinduism has, traditionally at least, had clearly set and defined roles for women within most sects, whereas Buddhism views both genders as fully equal and makes no distinctions between the two.

Chapter 6: Important Tips for Practicing Hinduism

Aside from the information presented in the previous chapters, you ought to know some valuable tips for the practice of Hinduism. These tips will serve as an essential guide in practicing this way of life. You can apply these tips whenever necessary.

1. **You may struggle to become a vegetarian, but don't give up**. In a carnivorous environment, becoming a vegetarian seems like a Herculean task, but don't despair. It will take time for your palate to adjust, but you will eventually succeed. Joining a Hindu group will make this task easier, but in such a case the oath of vegetarianism needs to be sacrosanct since it's a basic tenet of their way of life. However, if you already know vegetarianism to be beyond your reach, avoid larger organizations and approach smaller religio-cultural temple organizations which operate on local scales (especially if you manage to come across Bengali Hindu associations, which often embrace meat-eating more often than many other groups – even providing meats on days of prayers in some cases).

If you do attempt to turn vegetarian on you own, though, there are certain things you can do and keep in mind to help you. First and foremost, you should know that vegetarianism is far from being the most difficult diet to adhere to. Even if you forsake meat as a food source, you will still have an all but infinite assortment of highly nutritious as well as delicious foods.

Since adopting a vegetarian lifestyle is all about willpower and perseverance, there are plenty of facts and solid arguments in favor of such a choice, and you can use those to keep you motivated. Namely, one of the best arguments for vegetarianism is probably the health concerns associated with eating meat. Everybody knows that meat is a great source of protein, but what many people overlook is just how many fats it puts into your system. Many of these fats are not those good ones either. Instead, they are usually the main culprit with many forms of cardiovascular diseases which kill millions. Research is constantly producing increasingly solid evidence that meat consumption also increases our chances of acquiring diabetes and cancer among other illnesses as well.

Environmental and ethical issues associated with meat production and consumption is yet another side to the dice. For starters, horrific stories of systematic mistreatment and abuse of animals that are grown for the purpose of food are constantly cropping up. Without going into too much detail right now, this factor is definitely a useful thing to research on your own and use as a means of motivation. Not many people can remain indifferent to some of the conditions those animals live in.

As for the environmental aspect, you would no longer participate in an industry that uses staggering amounts of fresh water and other resources to produce disproportionally little pure meat. Either way, even if such knowledge doesn't prove enough to motivate you, you shouldn't be too hard on yourself as the pressure from the environment may sometimes be too much to bear. If the task proves impossible despite everything, you can look to religious groups that aren't too bent on vegetarianism, as I have mentioned.

Regardless, remember that Hinduism promotes a personal spiritual journey, regardless of the form which it may take. And so, if you believe yourself to be unable to fulfill the conditions of larger organizations, you can guide yourself along the spiritual path with the aid of the plethora of religious content available online. Along with teaching yourself the knowledge embedded within Hindu scriptures, you can also celebrate high holidays, host prayers, visit temples, and include yourself in any other Hindu activity which you would have enjoyed through a larger organization as well.

Hinduism is not a label or an official seal on your personality; it is merely a practice. Even if you don't adhere to every single principle, you can still say that you practice Hinduism. A Hindu is known by deeds before anything else, and these actions can often define you as one.

2. **There are numerous Hindu temples around the world.** Hence, you won't have a hard time finding one in your area, and participating in their activities. Google Search will help you find 'the way.'

If you don't have time to use search engines, you can copy and paste this, http://allhindutemples.com/, into your Internet's URL to access the Global Hindu Temples Directory. It's a list of the over 2,000 Hindu temples in more than 50 countries around the world.

The owner of this website, a design engineer named Hari Iyer, also developed a mobile application to help locate nearby Hindu temples wherever you may find yourself in the world. The app is a product of a diligent compilation of information on the many temples outside of India and Southeast Asia. The app provides its user with information such as address, phone number, as well as the hours when the temples are open to visitors and followers.

The information is lacking when it comes to India and Southeast Asia since those parts of the world are home to a huge number of temples, many of which are not very well represented online. Virtually anywhere else, though, the app can be used with your phone's location to detect temples in your close proximity automatically, if there are any. It's also possible to manually locate temples on the map and use a search system within the app.

3. **Studying the Bhagavad Gita and the Vedas entails a lot of hard work.** So, you must be

committed and dedicated to your conversion. Most of the time you'll be learning on your own. Hence, be positive about it, so that you can persevere and be self-motivated. Remember to have fun while learning, though.

The studying of the scripture is an integral part of the Hindu lifestyle, and it starts during formal education and continues for years. With some highly devoted individuals, studying the sacred texts is a lifetime task, just like in other major religions of the world. Of course, relative to your level of commitment and the goals you want to pursue with Hinduism, you may not want to delve into those depths. If this is the case, you can look for summarized and concise versions of some texts to help you get to the gist of the philosophies.

Just keep in mind that nobody masters the Hindu philosophies overnight, not even devout Hindus. You can approach your studies as a hobby, and within a few years of consistent learning, you may get to a significant level of knowledge.

4. **Meditation benefits those who hear it.** Therefore, it's important that you say the chant

out loud; just enough for people inside a small room to hear it, especially if it's a public chant. If you're alone, your voice should be soft but clearly audible to your own ear.

As part of group meditation, chants play an important role in developing the ambiance as well. It's important to contribute to the overall collective effort as well as to communicate to those situated close to you during the rituals. Chants and recitations all serve a very practical purpose in meditation, rites, and ceremonies and are definitely much more than a gimmick.

5. **Meditation can help decrease the risk of myocardial infarctions (heart attacks).** This is because it maintains the normal blood pressure and relaxes the body. This reduces stress that can trigger cardiac problems.

There are numerous medical researches and surveys that you can look up and see the observed health benefits of meditation for yourself. Those with high blood pressure, problems with sleeping, or regular stress can all benefit from regular meditative practices which usually take up about half an hour out of your day.

Apart from the strictly religious forms of meditation found in Hinduism, Buddhism, Jainism, and others, there are also quite a few methods and practices which anybody can take up regardless of religion. These range from specific techniques that you can conduct at home alone, which vary in complexity, to the simplest forms such as walking at a particularly easy pace through quiet parts while minding your breathing.

One well-known kind is what's often referred to as mindful meditation. This one is all about concentration and focus. You can assume a meditative posture and use a seemingly irrelevant object to focus on, which can be an actual, simple object, a specific word, or a mantra. The objective is to train yourself to direct all of your thoughts at one particular thing without interrupting your concentration. This is a good way to strengthen your mind and channel stressful and negative thoughts. Taking about half an hour every day to practice this can do wonders for both your mental and physical health.

6. **You can join yoga clubs to enhance your Bhakti yoga**. Yoga is important in Hinduism. It's one significant practice that people from Western countries choose to sign up for. It's because yoga doesn't only enhance your spiritual experience but

it also assists in maintaining a healthy mind and body.

Keep in mind that many people, particularly in the west, get into yoga without any aspirations towards converting to Hinduism, or any religion for that matter. These people are growing in numbers as well, with yoga already having a prominent place in popular culture. Apart from joining clubs and going to group yoga practice, it's also possible to hire a personal yoga trainer, or guru, to help you with the exercises. This can be a good way to learn about the history of the practices and other aspects of Hinduism too, especially if you get involved with Bhakti yoga in particular. Yoga is also known to go hand-in-hand with a vegetarian diet, and those two life choices, when working together, form the epitome of healthy living in modern times.

7. **"Conversion" to Hinduism is basically non-existent.** There are no formal conversion processes required by Hindu law that a person has to undergo. If a person wants to convert, the person simply has to sincerely change his way of life and adapt the Hindu way. The steps of conversion provided in Chapter 4 are the recommended steps based on the tenets of Vaishnavism. However, while Hinduism lacks the

clarity of a process similar to Christian Baptism –
visiting the temple of a deity of your choice,
requesting the priest to pray to him or her in your
name, and making an offering to the temple or to
the less fortunate after presenting it to your deity
often create an informal conversion of sorts.

Furthermore, remember that certain sects, such as
Vaishnavism, do offer initiation rituals to those
who want to go all the way with adopting the
Hindu way of life. Vaishnavism is also one of the
denominations that have strong representation
throughout the world, as shown by the example
of ISKCON. Such organizations will have within
their ranks some of those scholars who advocate
reforms concerning the controversial subject of
conversion. Thus, those movements may often be
much more open towards the idea of conversion
than others. At any rate, your best bet is always to
get in direct contact with your sect of interest and
just ask away.

8. **You can find Hinduism all around you.** The
   New World has discovered the power of yoga and
   meditation in boosting performance and
   productivity of individuals.

This is what I was referring to earlier. Hinduism and many of its practices have found their place in modern culture and even taken threads into medical fields, notably with therapeutic aspects of meditation. Everything points to the prospect of these philosophies spreading even further in the future, and with reform efforts within Hinduism itself, the religion and all of its wisdom are likely to become more and more accessible to a great number of people over time.

It isn't that uncommon for therapists to recommend various forms of meditation and yoga practices to their patients in the hopes of alleviating psychological or emotional problems. Such exercises may also be found in rehabilitation centers throughout the world. Many of these meditations and yoga methods can be traced back to traditions within Hinduism and other similar religions such as Buddhism.

9. **Take note that there are certain Hindus that don't accept the Vedas.** So don't be surprised if you meet someone in this category. There are numerous Hindu sects nowadays so there will be diversity in some of these numerous beliefs.

Hindu scriptures have been written down, especially the Vedas, fixed, enriched, and evolved for thousands of years, so it is natural that there will be variety like nowhere else. Make sure that you take notes from this book and do your diligence when approaching a sect or an organization. Read up on their specific beliefs and scriptures that the faith is based on.

Showing that you already possess the knowledge about the practices and origins of a particular sect, as well as having an understanding of the scriptures they follow, will go a long way towards your initiation into the sect. And if you are initiated, it will be easier to get a grasp of the basics and go on to the more advanced stages of learning.

10. **Gift giving during Diwali is customary.** So be ready with your gifts. You can conveniently shop online through Hindu websites for gifts made specifically for Diwali.

As part of ritual gift giving in Hinduism, you can't present the first thing you encounter and think will be of value. Specific kinds of gifts are presented to follow specific rituals. They are often highly symbolic and have great significance in the context of the religion. Denominations that strictly adhere to tradition will make the rules known, though, so this is another aspect that requires attention and studying.

Conclusion

Learning about Hinduism is a complex process because you have to be familiar with the Bhagavad Gita, the Vedas and the basic beliefs of Hindus. Understanding that Hinduism is a way of life will help you appreciate their religious scriptures and teachings with greater clarity.

In addition to the basic information provided in this book, you can further enrich your knowledge through the Sacred Texts. You can also start practicing Bhakti yoga (loving service) and meditation through the steps provided in this book. If you want to learn more quickly, you can enlist the help of a yoga teacher. There are also several online groups and applications that you can use to simplify the process.

If you want to convert, follow the recommended steps in this book and you won't go wrong. Of course, you can always modify the steps, if needed. You can be ingenious but still comply with the basic rules set in practicing the Hindu rituals, such as yoga.

Remember that many denominations of Hinduism started with people incorporating their own beliefs and traditions into the mix and fusing them with the existing Hindu principles. Hinduism is not a centralized religion with a clearly defined authoritative body that dictates the dogma, rituals, beliefs, and all the other aspects that define the particular faith. Instead, Hinduism is highly localized and open to all sorts of interpretations and adaptations. As long as the crucial tenets are observed, you will be able to call yourself a Hindu or at least a practicing Hindu.

Of course, it's not about the label. If you were not born into Hinduism, the chances are that you may get more value out of it by simply studying the philosophy and enriching your life with those principles you think would apply well to your life and improve your spiritual wellbeing.

It's also important to approach Hinduism with an open mind, especially if you come from a religious background. Of course, it's likely that your mind is already open if you chose to read about Hinduism, especially if you are interested in conversion. But it's worth mentioning that having no preconceived, personal notions and expectations is the best way to approach the teachings of this religion. Arguably, it may be particularly easy for Atheists and Agnostics to get into Hinduism, specifically due to the fact that most of the Hindu practices are known to be very accessible and suitable for those who have no belief in God.

If, however, you aspire to get thoroughly involved with Hinduism but come from a culture not rooted in the philosophy, your best bet is organizations such as ISKCON. The limits are very high to how far you can advance not only in your spiritual growth but with regards to your role in a particular sect as well. Such organizations are progressive and aim to promote Hinduism as a way of life, so their arms are very open to newcomers. Your personal initiative is everything, though, and it's crucial that you get deeply involved with the community and their practices.

With a lot of commitment to studying, practicing, and networking within the community, there really is no telling as to how far you can go along your Hindu path. Get informed about a particular organization's approach to initiation and discuss, with the priests and gurus, how you can help the cause and do your part. You never know, you may find a whole new purpose and end up playing a role in the sect you join.

Having thoroughly perused through the information in this book, it's time to put it all in action. Enjoy yourself, and bask in the resplendent incandescence of the Supreme Being above.

Finally, I'd like to thank you for purchasing this book! If you enjoyed it or found it helpful, I'd greatly appreciate it if you'd take a moment to leave a review on Amazon. Thank you!

Made in the USA
Lexington, KY
24 January 2017